LIONEL MESSI

www.pegasusforkids.com

© B. Jain Publishers (P) Ltd. All rights reserved. No part of this book may be reproduced, stored in a retrieval system or transmitted, in any form or by any means, mechanical, photocopying, recording or otherwise, without any prior written permission of the publisher.

Published by Kuldeep Jain for B. Jain Publishers (P) Ltd., D-157, Sector 63, Noida - 201307, U.P
Registered office: 1921/10, Chuna Mandi, Paharganj, New Delhi-110055

Printed in India

Contents

5   Who is Lionel Messi?

6   Birth and Early Life

11   Barcelona Calls

16   The Call Up

25   Best Player in the World

40   The Argentine National Team

64   Personal Life

71   Records, Awards and Recognition

75   Timeline

77   Activities

79   Glossary

Who is Lionel Messi?

Lionel Andrés Messi is an Argentine footballer who plays for FC Barcelona in Spain at club level. He is also the Captain of the Argentine national football team. Popularly known as Leo Messi, he is quite often regarded as the best player in the world and is arguably one of the best players to have ever played the game.

Messi remains the only player in the history of football to have won five FIFA Ballon D'Or Awards (World Player of the Year), four of which he won back-to-back. He is also the first player to win three European Golden Boot Awards (European Top Scorer). With his club Barcelona, Messi has won the Spanish League title eight times, the UEFA Champions League four times and the Copa Del Rey four times as well.

A truly gifted footballer, Messi is a prolific goal scorer and a creative playmaker with a knack for achieving the extraordinary, time and time again. He also holds the record for the most league goals scored in a single Spanish League Season (50), in a calendar year (91), in one football season (82), as well as the record for most assists made in the Spanish League and the Copa America Tournament. These extraordinary numbers not only underline the sheer brilliance of the person but also make him one of the greatest sportspersons in history.

Birth and Early Life

Born on June 24, 1987 in Rosario, Argentina, Lionel Messi was the third of four children born to Jorge Messi and Celia Cuccittini. His father was a steel factory manager and

his mother worked at a magnet manufacturing workshop. He was raised in a tight-knit, football-loving family. Messi developed a passion for football in his childhood and played regularly with his brothers, Matias and Rodrigo,

his cousins, as well as with other children in his locality. At the age of four, Messi joined a local club 'Grandoli', where his father coached him. His earliest influence to play football came from his maternal grandmother, Celia, who accompanied Messi to his games and showed keen interest in her grandson's career. Sadly, when she passed away before his eleventh birthday, he was greatly affected. Since then, he has celebrated each one of his goals by looking up and pointing towards the sky—a tribute to his grandmother.

Messi joined his hometown club 'Newell's Old Boys' at the age of six. For six years, he played at the Rosario-based club, scoring almost 500 goals for 'The Machine of 87', the nearly unbeatable youth team named after the year of the team members' birth.

At the age of ten, Messi was diagnosed with a growth hormone deficiency, which hindered his physical growth and threatened to end his career in its early stages. His father's health insurance only covered two years of his medical treatment, which cost USD 1,000 a month. At first, Newell's agreed to help with his treatment, but later backed out. Around the same time, Leo was scouted by star player Pablo Aimar of the famous Buenos Aires Club River Plate. Aimar was someone Messi idolised. However, due to Argentina's economic collapse at that time, the club was unable to help him with his treatment. The search to seek help for their son's treatment brought the Messi family to Barcelona, Spain.

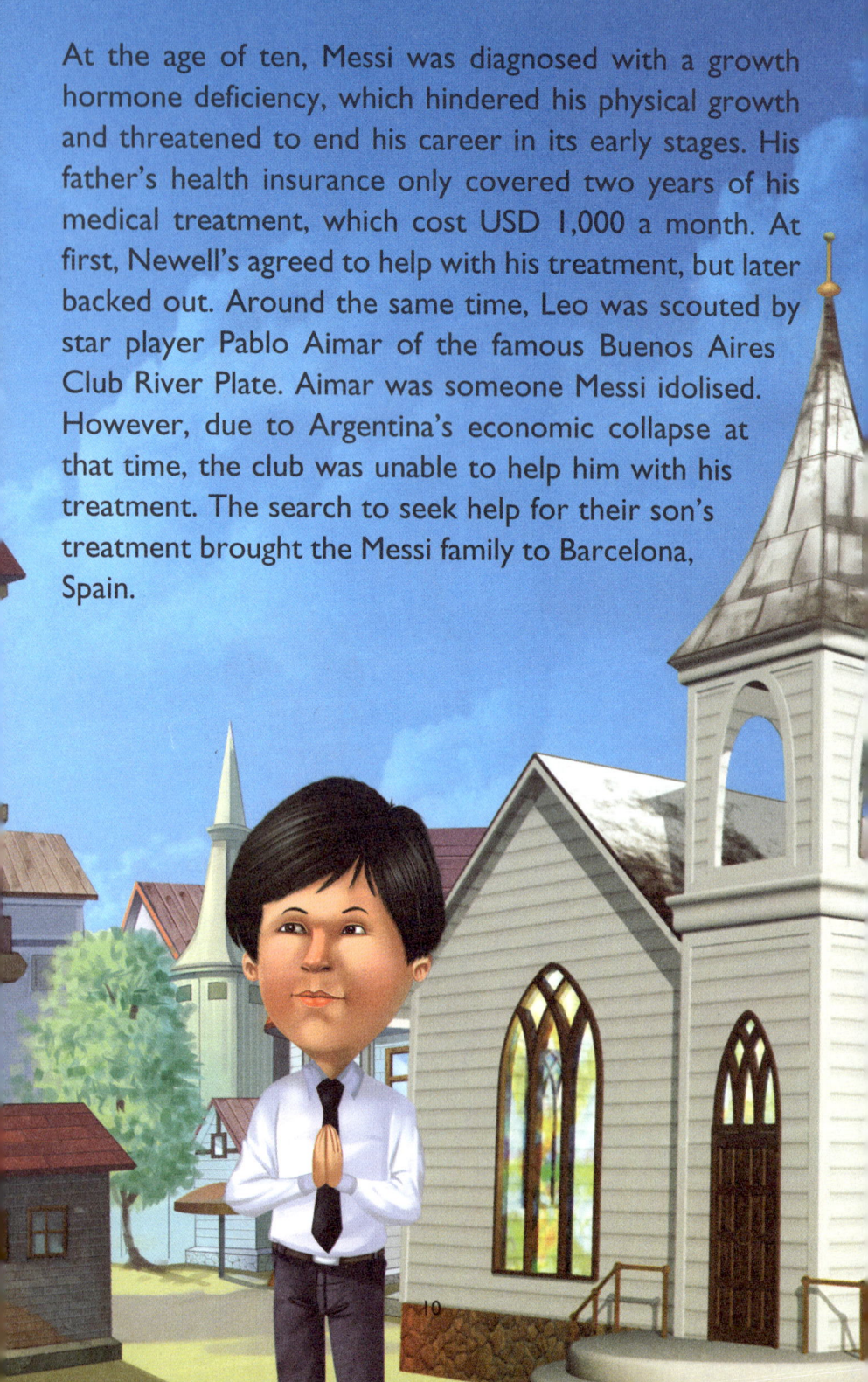

Barcelona Calls

The Messi family had relatives in Catalonia, Spain. They succeeded in setting up a trial with FC Barcelona in September 2000. The club's first team director, Charly Rexach, immediately talked to the board of directors about signing up young Leo. However, they hesitated, as it was unusual at the time for European clubs to sign such

young foreign players. On December 14, 2000, the family gave Barcelona an ultimatum to prove their commitment. With no proper documents or stationery at hand, Rexach offered Messi a contract on a paper napkin. Thus, in February 2001, the Messi family shifted to Barcelona, into an apartment near the club's stadium, Camp Nou.

During his first year in Spain, Messi hardly played for the youth side due to a transfer conflict with Newell, his former team. As a foreigner, he was only eligible to play in friendlies and the Catalan League. This made it difficult for him to adapt to the style of play of his new team. Messi was a very reserved person and the lack of interaction with his new teammates made them think that he might be mute. Personally, he suffered from homesickness since his mother had moved back to Argentina with his brothers and little sister, while he stayed back in Barcelona with his father.

For one year, Messi was enrolled at the Barcelona Youth Academy, 'La Masia'. In February 2002, Messi was finally registered in the Royal Spanish Football Federation. This meant that he was finally eligible to play in all competitions. It was now, at the age of 14, that he finally completed his growth hormone treatment.

Messi soon found great friends in his teammates, Francesc Fabregas and Gerard Pique. By then he also became a very important player of 'The Baby Dream Team', FC Barcelona's best ever youth team. During his first full season in 2002–2003, Messi was the youth side's top scorer with 30 goals in 36 matches. As a result of his extraordinary scoring feats, his youth team 'Cadentes A' won three major tournaments—the League, the Spanish and Catalan Cup trophies. Towards the end of that season, Messi had an offer from the English club Arsenal FC, to join them. It was his first transfer offer from a foreign club. Though Fabregas and Pique chose to leave, Messi decided to stay on with Barcelona.

The Call Up

In 2003-2004, Lionel Messi played his fourth season with Barcelona. It was during this season that Messi really took off, rapidly progressing through the club ranks and making a name for himself in the youth teams. He debuted a record five times in this one season—in the Juvenile B, Juvenile A, Barcelona First Team, Barcelona B and Barcelona C teams.

Messi was named the player of the tournament in four international pre-season tournaments while playing for the 'Juvenile B' team. As a result of his excellent performances in the pre-season, he was promoted to the 'Juvenile A' team, where he scored a whopping 18 goals in 11 league matches. He was one of the several youth team players called to add to a depleted First Team of the

season. On November 16, 2003, at 16 years of age, Lionel Messi made his First Team debut when he came on as a substitute in the seventy fifth minute against FC Porto. His performance in that game, creating two chances and a shot on target, impressed the coaching staff. From this point on, Messi began training with the First Team once a week and with 'Barcelona B' on a daily basis. On his first day of training with the First Team, almost everyone noticed his tremendous talent and the huge efforts he made to keep improving his game.

Barcelona's star player, Ronaldinho, noticed Messi's potential. He is known to have commented that the young Argentine would go on to become a better player than himself. Ronaldinho played a vital role in Messi's spectacular rise, mentoring him during his crucial developing years and easing his transition into the first team.

The same year, Messi started to play for 'Barcelona C' to gain valuable match experience. He played his first for Barcelona C on November 29, 2003. Due to his excellent performances, he helped the third team from being relegated to the third division. He scored five goals in 10 appearances, which included a brilliant hat trick in the Spanish Cup game against Sevilla.

Though he was mentally strong, Messi was physically weaker than his opponents. He had to take extra training for his muscles to become stronger. By the end of the season, Messi returned for both the Barcelona 'B' and 'C' teams and scored 36 goals for them in all competitions as the season came to a close.

The next year, in 2004-2005, Messi emerged as an important part of the B team. He played 17 times and scored six goals for the reserve side. Although he had debuted with the first team in the previous season, Messi had not played any matches for them subsequently. However, his performance during training impressed the other first team players to such an extent that they convinced the manager, Frank Rijkaard, to promote Messi to the first team. Since Ronaldinho already played on the left side, Messi, against his wishes, was shifted to the right side of the field, a position that was not his strongest point. Nonetheless, like all great players, he adapted well and overcame the challenges put in front of him.

Messi made his league debut against RCD Espanyol on October 16, 2004 as a substitute in the 82nd minute of the game. This meant that Messi was the youngest-ever player to represent FC Barcelona in an official competition. At the time, Messi was just 17 years, three months and 22 days old, and he played 77 minutes in nine matches for the first team that season. In the same year, he also made his UEFA Champions League debut against FC Shaktar Donetsk.

Messi scored his first goal for Barcelona on May 1, 2005 against Albacete Balompié, SAD, assisted by Ronaldinho, and became the club's youngest scorer ever. His first goal was a telling point for him and also for the club's future, as it set up the emerging star's era of domination in the coming seasons.

Best Player in the World

Messi slowly but steadily became a household name the world over. In the 2005-2006 season, he was given the number 19 jersey and started playing in the right wing, forming a lethal attacking partnership with fellow teammates Ronaldinho and Samuel Eto'o.

Messi was now a regular for the first team and even started playing major games against arch rival, Real Madrid CF. He helped his team win against Chelsea FC in the UEFA Champions League, which was his best performance for FC Barcelona till then. He scored eight goals in 25 matches, which included his first goal in the Champions League.

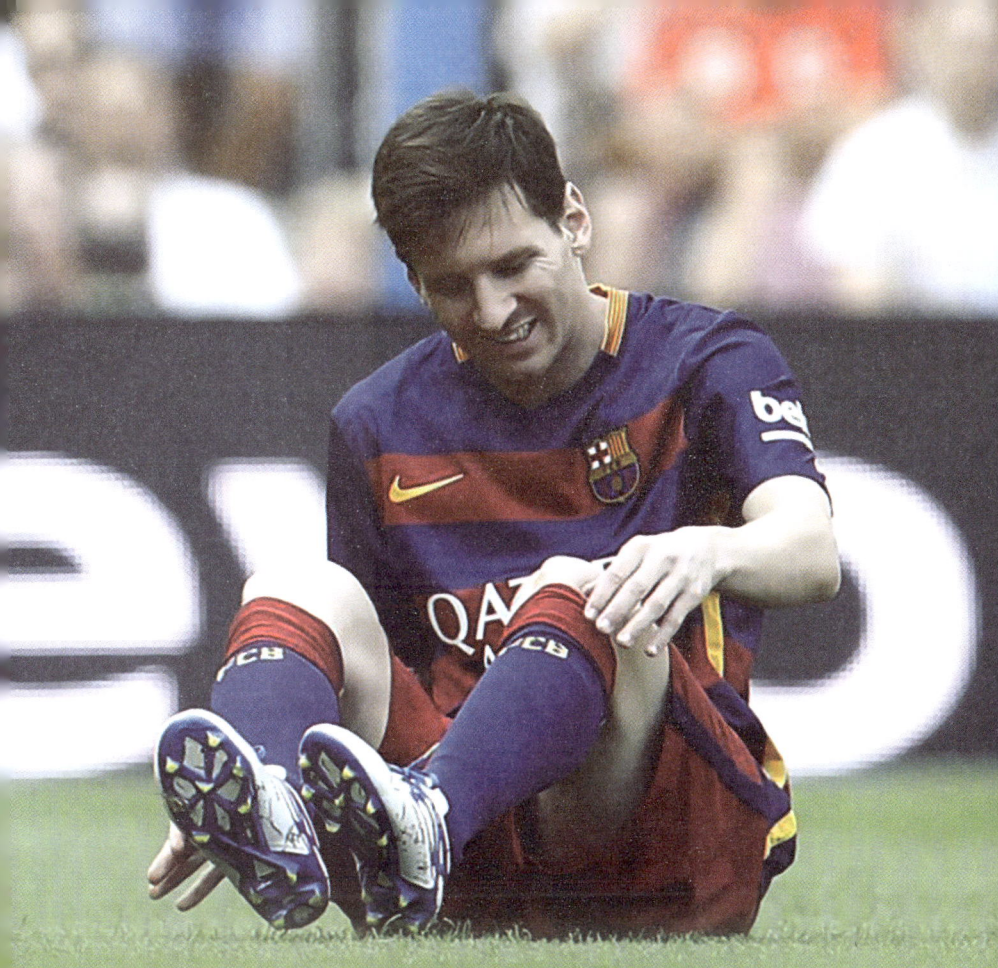

However, Messi's impressive campaign with Barcelona that season came to a premature end when he injured himself in the second half of the semi final against Chelsea on May 7, 2006. Despite his best efforts, Messi was unable to regain full fitness, and was told that he could not play in the Champions League final against Arsenal. His absence in that match inspired Barcelona to play even harder, and as a result they triumphed, winning the final. It was their first Champions League trophy after 14 years, and young Messi's first of many to come.

The season after winning the Champions League title, Barcelona underwent an unusual decline in form. Their playing methods became too predictable, and their players failed to perform at the level that had won them trophies in the earlier seasons. Despite all the club's hardships on the field, it was in this season that Lionel Messi established himself as one of the best players in the world.

By then Messi had a strong fan following as people realised that a player of his ability came around only once or twice in a decade. He scored 17 goals in 36 appearances across all competitions that season. He was still not free of the 'injury curse' and sustained major injuries before and during crucial matches. His injuries proved costly for Barcelona, as they were knocked out of the Champions League by Liverpool FC and lost the league title.

When Messi finally returned after a lengthy injury lay off, he made an instant impact by scoring 11 goals in the last 13 league matches of the season. But despite his best efforts, Barcelona could not win any trophies that season.

The highlight of Barcelona and Messi's season was the 'El Clasico' match between Barcelona and Real Madrid on March 10, 2007, where Messi scored his first hat trick for Barcelona. He thus became the first player in 12 years to score a hat trick in the El Clasico. His stellar display silenced his critics who had questioned the youngster's ability.

In 2007–2008, Ronaldinho lost his sparkling form and the team became increasingly dependent on Messi. At a mere

20 years of age, Messi thrived under this new pressure. His spectacular performances earned him the name 'Messiah' from the Spanish media after he almost single-handedly won matches for Barcelona. His performance that season earned him global recognition from fans as well as worldwide media. He was nominated for the Ballon D'Or in 2007 alongside Cristiano Ronaldo and Ricardo Kaka, although he finished third that year. This formed a career defining point for Lionel Messi. From here onwards, his performances grew from strength to strength.

Meanwhile, in 2008 Barcelona manager, Frank Rijkaard, was replaced by Josep 'Pep' Guardiola, a former Captain of the Barcelona team. He brought in a whole new sports philosophy and introduced the 'Tiki-Taka' technique of play. This involved frequent movement of the midfielders and sharp one-touch passing.

This was also the season when Barcelona bid farewell to the iconic Ronaldinho. Messi now inherited the legendary 'number 10' jersey and also signed a new contract in July 2008, which made him the club's highest paid player.

In the first season under Pep Guardiola, Messi frequently switched positions between the right wing and the central attacking midfield, which allowed him more freedom. He was able to create more goal scoring chances and have an even greater impact on the outcome of the matches due to this new found freedom on the field.

Further, Messi was put under a completely different training regime and nutrition plan. He was also assigned a personal trainer who would travel with him to all the matches. As a result, Messi stayed almost injury-free for the next four years, which allowed him to reach his full potential. In his first injury-free season, Messi scored 38 goals in just 51 matches across all competitions. The newly formed attacking trio of Thiery Henry, Samuel Eto'o and Leo Messi scored a club record of 100 goals that season.

Messi played his first major final since breaking into the first team on May 13, 2008 in the Copa Del Rey final against Atheltic Bilbao. He scored one goal as well as assisted his

team's second goal in the 4-1 victory. Barcelona also won the La Liga title, where Messi scored 23 goals in the league. Messi scored nine goals in the UEFA Champions League that season, becoming the competition's youngest-ever top scorer. He returned to the central attacking midfield position in the final of the Champions League against the English Champions—Manchester United FC—where he scored a brilliant headed goal in the 2-0 victory and earned himself and the club its second Champions League Trophy in four years.

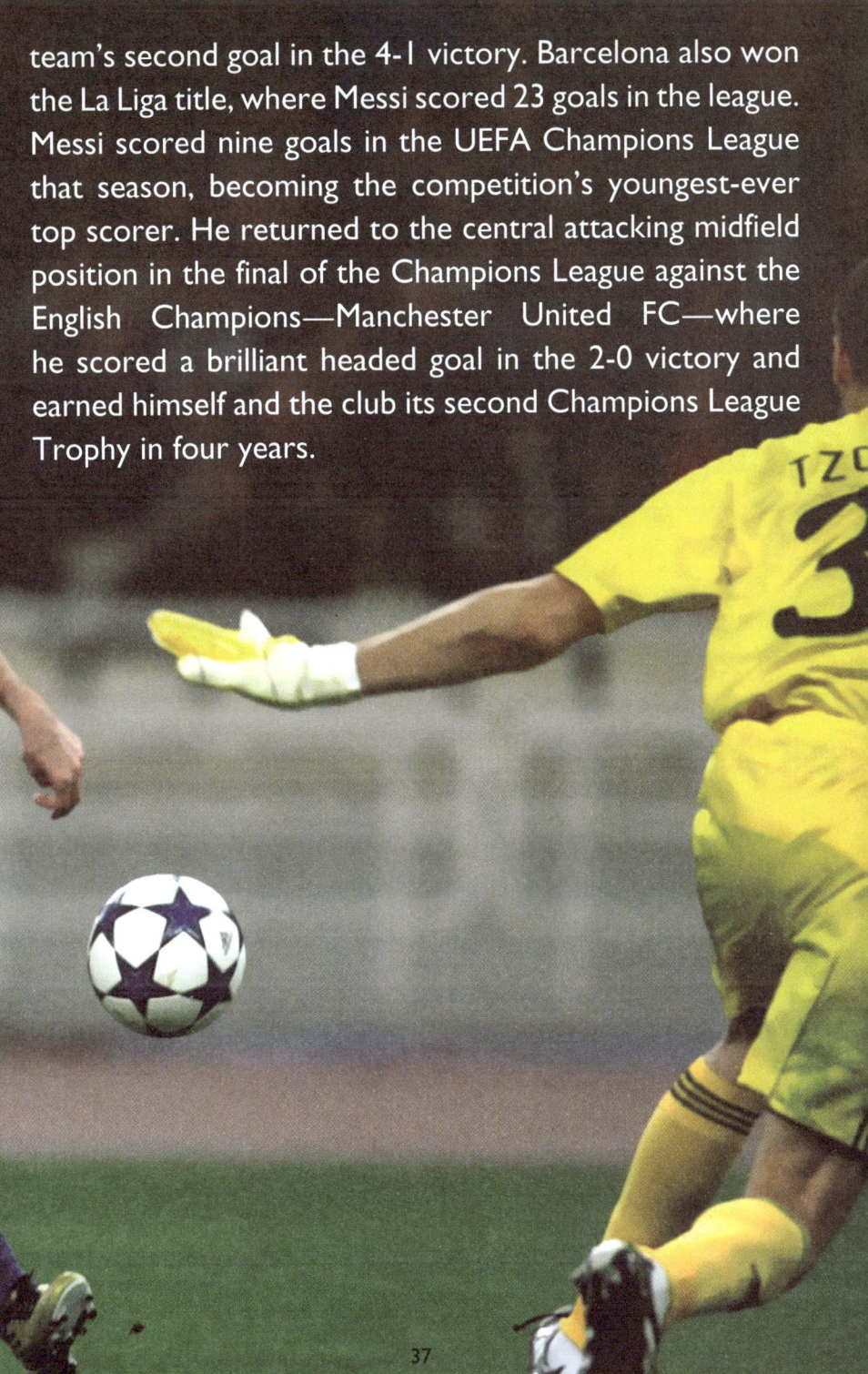

Despite his brilliant performances that season, Messi was yet again unable to win the Ballon D'Or in 2008, after finishing as runner up to Cristiano Ronaldo.

Barcelona had become the First Team in the history of Spanish football to win three major trophies in a single season (2008-2009). Their success continued into the second half of 2009, when they won the UEFA Super Cup,

Supercopa De Espana and FIFA World Cup, becoming the first-ever team to win all six trophies in a calendar year.

After achieving such incredible success in a short span of time and also due to his consistently brilliant performances on the field, Lionel Messi finally won his first Ballon D'Or in 2009, by the greatest voting margin in the competition's history.

The Argentine National Team

Leo Messi had to make a choice between Argentina and Spain when it came to playing at the international level. As he had dual citizenship, he was eligible to play for either of the two countries. While both countries were desperate to have him in their team, Messi chose to represent Argentina, the country of his birth.

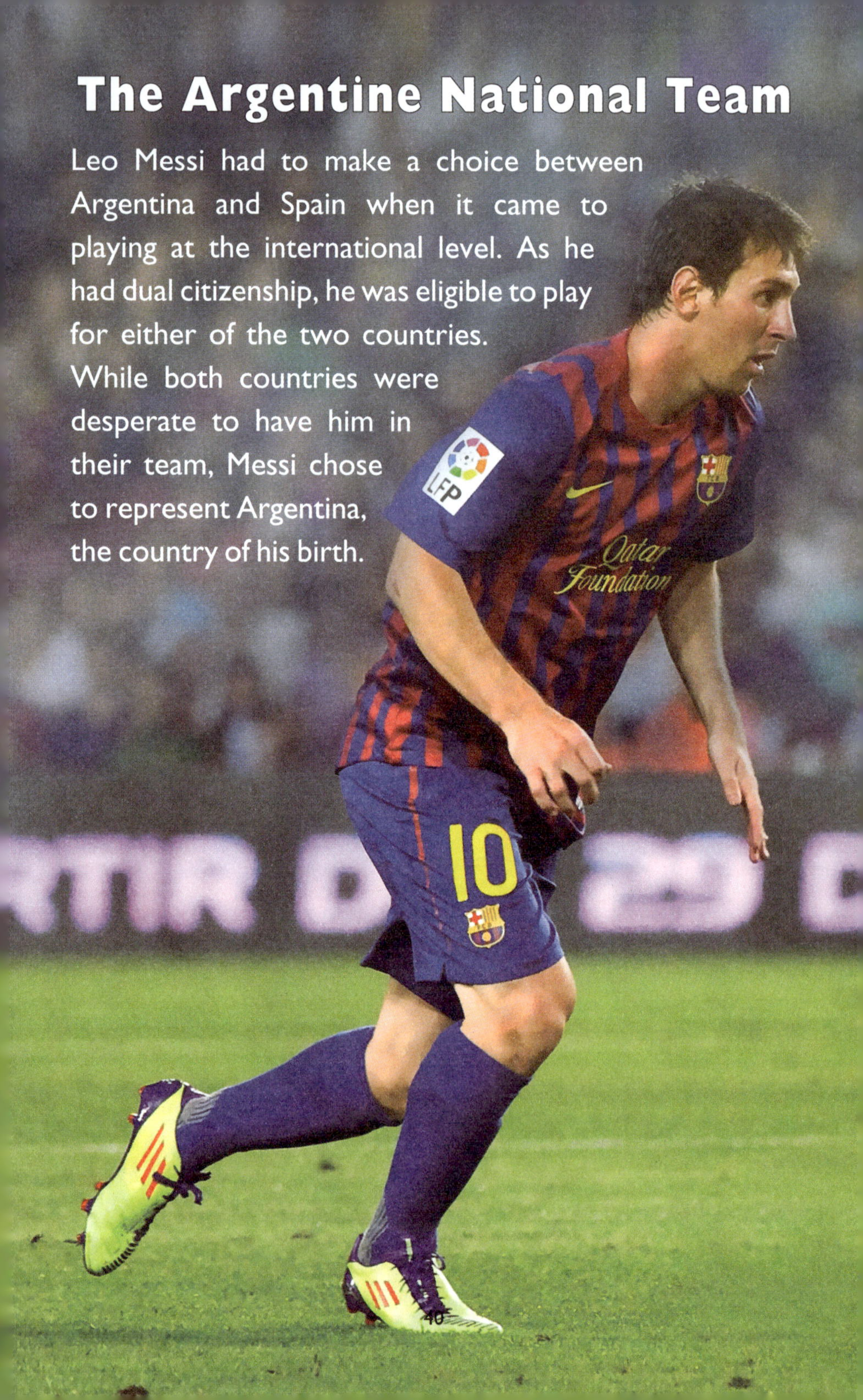

Messi made his international debut with the junior team on June 29, 2005, at the age of 17, against Paraguay, scoring one goal and providing two assists in an incredible 8-0 victory. Prior to this, his first major tournament for Argentina was the South American Youth Championships held in Colombia in February 2005. He was named 'Man of the Match' in the match against Venezuela; he also scored the winning goal in a 2-1 win against Brazil in their last match of the tournament, securing third place qualification for the summer's FIFA World Youth Championship.

The World Youth Championship was held in the Netherlands in June 2005. Messi was not part of the starting line-up in the first game of the tournament against USA, which Argentina lost 1-0. This led the senior players of the team to approach the coach and request him to let Messi start the remaining matches as he was their best player. Thus, Messi started the remainder of the games and made an instant impact, helping the team defeat Germany and Egypt. They were now in the knockout stages. Messi proved to be the telling difference in these stages, scoring the equaliser against Colombia by providing an assist and scoring one goal against title favourites Spain. He also scored the opening goal against the defending champions and Argentina's arch rivals, Brazil. His goal scoring exploits continued till the final, where he scored two penalties against Nigeria, securing Argentina their fifth FIFA World Youth Championship title. Messi was awarded the 'Golden Ball' as the best player in the tournament and the 'Golden Boot' for being the top scorer of the tournament with six goals.

In August 2005, Leo Messi was selected to join the senior national team by First Team manager Jose Pekerman. Thus, Messi made his senior Argentina debut on August 17, 2005 at the age of 18. Following his debut, he featured regularly for them in the build up to the 2006 FIFA World Cup in Germany.

Messi scored his first goal for the Argentine national team on March 1, 2005 in a friendly match against Croatia. In the first game of the World Cup in Germany, Messi watched from the bench as Argentina defeated Ivory Coast in their opening group game of the tournament. In the second game against Montenegro, Messi entered

in the seventy-fourth minute and became the youngest player to represent Argentina at the World Cup. He

provided an assist within minutes of his entry and scored his team's sixth goal in the impressive 6-0 win. This also made him the youngest scorer in the tournament and the sixth youngest goal scorer in the history of the World Cup.

Messi started the next game against Netherlands after several First Team players were rested, playing out a 0-0 draw and topping their group. On his nineteenth birthday, Messi played against Mexico in the 'round of 16' match where he entered as substitute in the eighty-fourth minute and eventually helped his team win the game in extra time. Despite his increasingly impressive performances, Messi did not feature in the quarterfinal match against Germany, where Argentina was defeated 4-2 due to penalties, and was knocked out of the World Cup.

In 2008, Messi travelled to Beijing with the Argentine team to represent his country in the Olympics. It came as no surprise when Messi, yet again, starred in Argentina's 2-1 win against Ivory Coast scoring the opening goal and setting up the second. Argentina ensured their qualification to the next round following a 1-0 victory over Australia in their last group game against Serbia. Though Messi was rested, Argentina won the match and finished top of the group. Once he was back in the starting line-up against Netherlands, he scored the first goal again and assisted

the second one as Argentina came out victorious after extra time. In the semi final, Argentina made an important statement after they humiliated Brazil with a 3-0 win and advanced to the finals where they were to face Nigeria. Messi assisted the only goal in the final against Nigeria, thus leading Argentina to win the Olympic Gold Medal. Along with fellow teammate, Juan Roman Riquelme, he was included in the 'team of the tournament', which further underlined his status as one of the best players in the world.

In 2010, Messi represented Argentina in his second FIFA World Cup campaign held in South Africa. The Argentine team was coached by the legendary former player and captain of the Argentina team, Diego Maradona. Despite their poor qualifying campaign, Argentina won all three of their group games and qualified for the knockout stages where they faced Mexico. Argentina defeated them 3-1 with Messi creating one goal and scoring another. In their

next match against Germany, however, Messi was tightly marked by the opposing team, preventing him from having any real impact on the game. Argentina lost 4-0 and returned home.

The unsuccessful World Cup stint was followed by the defeat in Copa America, where Argentina was knocked out in the quarter finals by rival Uruguay in a penalty shootout, despite Messi's best efforts to carry his country forward.

After two unsuccessful major tournaments in as many years, Argentina appointed Alejandro Sabella as their coach. Sabella's first act as coach of the national team was appointing Messi as the Captain. The captaincy proved to give a reserved Messi an extra push and motivation to show the world his love and passion for the sport. Sabella played Messi in the central attacking midfield, his preferred position. It was then that Messi really flourished and played exceptionally well for his country. His goal scoring increased significantly—he scored 25 times in 32 appearances for his country.

In 2012, Messi achieved yet another record when he scored a total of 12 goals in a single calendar year for his country, equalling the record set by Gabriel Batistuta, Argentina's all time top-scorer. On February 29, 2012, Messi scored his first hat trick for Argentina in a friendly match against Switzerland. This was followed by another

two hat tricks, against Brazil and Guatemala. Messi then helped Argentina qualify for the 2014 FIFA World Cup with a 5-2 victory against Paraguay where he provided,

assisted and scored twice from the penalty spot. In the qualification campaign, Messi had scored 10 goals in 14 matches for Argentina, a far cry from his previous, so-called 'mediocre' performances for the national team. This proved to be a turning point in Argentina's as well as Messi's fortunes.

The 2014 World Cup in Brazil was Messi's first as Captain of the national team, a role he cherished and excelled at. In the opening game against Bosnia & Herzegovina, Messi scored and assisted in a 2-1 win. The second game against Iran saw him score an outrageous goal from 25 yards in the dying moments of the game. In the last game of the group against Nigeria, Messi scored twice in a 3-2 win.

Argentina then faced Switzerland in the round of sixteen clash or the knock out stages. Yet again, Messi proved to be the winning difference as he created the only goal of the game. He was named as the 'Man of the Match' in each of Argentina's first four matches in the tournament.

The final was renamed as 'Messi versus Germany' by football fans around the world, as the best player in the world was to go up against the best team in the world. However, despite Messi's stellar performance, Argentina lost the match when German substitute, Mario Gotze, scored the winning goal in the 113rd minute of extra

time. The Germans won the World Cup 1-0, which was heartbreaking for Messi. As proved by his extraordinary efforts to carry his team all the way to the final, Lionel Messi was voted as the best player of the tournament, and was awarded the Golden Ball in recognition of his incredible performances at the FIFA World Cup.

Soon after, Messi led the national team in the 2015 Copa America held in Chile. Argentina faced competition from Paraguay, Uruguay and Jamaica to finish the group as a winner. When playing against Jamaica, Messi created Argentine National Team's history by becoming the fifth player to make a hundred appearances for the team. In the quarter finals, Colombia's goalkeeper David Ospina blocked Messi and his teammates on several occasions in the game. As a result, Argentina had to go to a penalty shootout to finally win the match by 5-4.

Next, Messi scored three goals and assisted in three more against Paraguay to win by 6-1 and advance to the finals. Argentina and Messi received much praise for their performance from what was initially a hostile crowd. They faced the host, Chile, in the final and after a goalless match, Chile beat Argentina by 4-1 in the penalty shootout. Yet again, Messi could not win the final for Argentina. Despite losing two major finals in two years, Messi was praised by his teammates, coaches and countrymen as he evolved into a genuine leader.

The next year, in 2016, Messi once again led the Argentine team in the 'Copa America Centenario'. In the second match, Messi scored a hat trick against Panama, leading Argentina to a 5-0 victory. Messi was named 'Man of the Match', and Argentina advanced to the quarter finals.

On June 18, 2016, in the quarter final against Venezuela, Messi put in yet another match winning display, creating two goals and scoring another in a 4-1. This saw him equal Gabriel Batistuta's record of 54 goals in official international games. He then broke that record in the 4-0 semi final win against USA where he scored a stunning free kick, and was named 'Man of the Match' once again.

In a repeat of the previous year's final, Argentina faced Chile. Despite their best efforts, however, Argentina lost in the penalty shootout by 4-1. This was Messi's fourth loss in a major tournament final, and his third in a row. After the final against Chile on June 26, 2016, Messi announced his retirement from the Argentina National Team.

Personal Life

Despite living in constant glare of the media, Messi has done a remarkable job of keeping his personal life, especially his family and friends, away from the limelight.

Messi has a close relationship with his family members, especially his mother. He has a tattoo on his left shoulder in her honour. His father, Jorge, looks after his career and has been his agent since Messi was 14 years old. His daily affairs, schedules and publicity are handled by his elder brother Rodrigo. Messi's mother, Celia, and his other brother, Matias, manage the superstar's charity organisation, the 'Leo Messi Foundation', and also take care of his private and professional matters in Argentina.

Messi is in a relationship with his childhood sweetheart, Antonella Rocuzzo, who belongs to his hometown of Rosario. They have known each other since they were children, and have been together since Messi was 20 years old. They have two sons together—Thiago, who was born on November 2, 2012, and Mateo, who was born on September 11, 2015. Leo has a tattoo of his elder son Thiago's name and handprint on his left calf.

Despite the tremendous international success and adulation from fans and media around the world, Messi has never lost touch with his roots. He was a shy and reserved person from the beginning, and he remains grounded and humble even today—two qualities that make him not only an amazing player but a good person.

Messi remains close with his friends back home as well. Many of these were his teammates from the 'Machine of '87' at Newell's Old Boys. Although Messi has spent practically his whole career playing with just one club—Barcelona—he has always hinted that he would like to return to Newell one day, to end his career where it all began.

Apart from being an excellent player, Messi has also proved himself as a good human being. He has been regularly associated with charity work throughout his career. He is particularly involved with charitable actions towards underprivileged and ill children. Since 2004, Messi has contributed his time and money towards the United Nations Children's Fund (UNICEF), which also has a strong bond with FC Barcelona. Messi was made

global ambassador of UNICEF in 2010. He took part in his first mission afterwards when he travelled to Haiti to raise global awareness about the massive destruction and hardships faced by the country. Messi has since been a part of several UNICEF campaigns and missions, which have targeted prevention of diseases among underprivileged children, the importance of education, and social inclusion of disabled children.

In 2007, an incident affected Messi deeply. He visited a hospital for terminally ill children in his hometown of

Rosario. While spending time with these children, he was moved by their plight and decided to form a charitable organisation that focused on giving proper healthcare, education, food, shelter and sporting facilities to children around the world. This organisation came to be known as the 'Leo Messi Foundation'. Through his foundation, Messi has funded research, financed medical training, and also helped build hospitals and medical clinics in Argentina, Spain and also in other parts of the world.

His humility, respect and philanthropy along with his incredible and extraordinary achievements on the football field have made Messi arguably the greatest player ever in the history of the game.

Since his debut for FC Barcelona, Messi has broken several international football records and set new ones.

Club Awards:

- 8 La Liga (Spanish League) titles
- 4 UEFA Champions League titles
- 4 Copa Del Rey titles
- 3 FIFA Club World Cup titles

International Honours:

- FIFA World Youth Championship 2005: Winners
- Olympic Gold Medal 2008
- FIFA World Cup 2014: Runner-up
- Copa America 2007, 2015, 2016: Runner-up

Individual Awards:

- FIFA Ballon D'Or Winner: 2009, 2010, 2011, 2012, 2015
- UEFA Club Footballer of the Year: 2009
- UEFA Best Player in Europe: 2011, 2015
- European Golden Shoe: 2010, 2012, 2013
- La Liga Best Player: 2009, 2010, 2011, 2012, 2013, 2015

Records, Awards and Recognition

- Argentina Footballer of the Year: 2005, 2007, 2008, 2009, 2010, 2011, 2012, 2013, 2015
- FIFA World Cup Golden Ball: 2014
- FIFA FIFPro World Eleven: 2007, 2008, 2009, 2010, 2011, 2012, 2013, 2014, 2015
- UEFA Team of the Year: 2008, 2009, 2010, 2011, 2012, 2014, 2015
- FIFA World Cup Dream Team: 2014
- La Liga Team of the Year: 2015
- Copa America Dream Team: 2007, 2011, 2015, 2016
- UEFA Goal of the Year: 2007, 2015
- FIFPro World Young Player of the Year: 2006, 2007, 2008
- FIFA World Youth Championship Golden Ball: 2005
- FIFA World Youth Championship Golden Boot: 2005
- La Liga Top Scorer: 2009-2010, 2011-2012, 2012-2013
- La Liga Top Assists Provider: 2010-2011, 2014-15, 2015-2016
- UEFA Champions League Top Scorer: 2008-2009,

2009-2010, 2010-2011, 2011-2012, 2014-2015
- UEFA Champions League Top Assists Provider: 2011-2012, 2014-2015
- Copa America Top Assists Provider: 2011, 2015, 2016

Records:

- Most FIFA Ballon D'Or Awards: 2009-2012, 2015
- Youngest Ballon D'Or Two Time and Three Time Winner: 23 and 24 years old
- Most UEFA Player of the Year Awards: 3 (2009, 2011, 2015)
- Most La Liga Best Player Awards: 6 (2009-2013, 2015)
- Top La Liga Goal Scorer: 312 Goals
- Top La Liga Assists: 127 Assists
- Most Goals in El Clasico: 21 Goals
- Most Goals for Club and Country in a Calendar Year: 91 Goals in 2012
- Most Goals for Club in all Competitions in a Single Season: 73 Goals in 2011-2012
- Most Goals for Club in all Competitions in a Calendar Year: 79 Goals in 2012

Records, Awards and Recognition

- Top Goal-scorer in a La Liga Season: 50 Goals in 2011-2012
- Most Hattricks Scored in a La Liga Season: 8 in 2011-2012
- Youngest Player to Score 200 Goals in La Liga: 23 years old
- Most Hattricks in the UEFA Champions League: 5
- Most Goals Scored in A UEFA Champions League Match: 5 Goals
- Youngest Player to Make 100 Appearances in UEFA Champions League: 28 years old (2015)
- Most Titles Won With Barcelona: 28
- Barcelona's Top-scorer: 477 Goals
- Barcelona's Top-scorer in UEFA Champions League: 82 Goals
- Most Hat tricks by a Barcelona Player: 35
- Argentina National Team's Top Scorer: 55 Goals
- Youngest Player to Play for Argentina in FIFA World Cup: 18 years, 357 days old (2006)
- Youngest Player to Score for Argentina in FIFA World Cup: 18 years, 357 years of age (2006)
- Youngest Player to Appear 100 Times for a Country: 27 years, 361 years old (2015)

Timeline

- **1987** Lionel Messi was born in Rosario, Argentina
- **1994** Joined hometown club Newell's Old Boys
- **2000** Diagnosed with growth hormone deficiency disease
- **2001** Relocated to Barcelona with his father and signed with FC Barcelona
- **2003** Made his senior team debut for Barcelona
- **2004** Signed his first professional contract and made his league debut for Barcelona; made his UEFA Champions League debut
- **2005** Scored his first senior goal for FC Barcelona; won his first league title with FC Barcelona; made his debut for Argentina; won the FIFA Youth World Championship for Argentina
- **2006** Won his first UEFA Champions League with FC Barcelona; made his first appearance in the FIFA World Cup
- **2007** Chosen in the FIFA world team of the year; Argentina Player of the Year; awarded UEFA Goal of the Year title; FIFPro Young Player of the Year

Timeline

- **2008** Won the Gold Medal with Argentina in the Olympics
- **2009** Won his first FIFA Ballon D'Or; part of the winning team for the UEFA Champions League; top scorer in the UEFA Champions League; La Liga Best Player
- **2010** Won his second FIFA Ballon D'Or
- **2011** Won his third consecutive Ballon D'Or; made Captain of the Argentina National Team
- **2012** Birth of his son, Thiego; won his fourth consecutive Ballon D'Or; scored a world record breaking 91 goals in a calendar year
- **2013** Youngest player to score 100 goals in La Liga
- **2014** Led Argentina to the FIFA World Cup final; named Best Player in the World Cup; won the Golden Ball
- **2015** Birth of his second son, Mateo; won his historic fifth Ballon D'Or
- **2016** Argentina's all time top scorer; announced retirement from the Argentina national team

Class Discussion

Why are sports important for us?

Debate on the topic: Should sports be given equal importance as studies?

Group Activity

Make a presentation on your favourite sportsperson or team. You can take up any sportsperson of your choice.

Conduct research about the different types of tournaments and leagues in international football.

Activities

Questions

1. Where was Lionel Messi born?

2. What is Messi's full name?

3. Which was the First Team he played for?

4. Why did he move to Spain?

5. At what age did he play his first game for Barcelona?

6. When did he score his first goal for Barcelona?

7. When did he win his first Ballon D'Or (Player of the year) trophy?

8. How many Ballon D'Or trophies has Messi won?

9. When was he made the captain of the Argentina National Team?

10. Messi holds the record for the most goals in a calendar year. How many goals has he scored in a calendar year and in which year did he score them?

assist: a pass that leads to a goal being scored

attacker: a player who leads the ball towards the opponent's goal area, to create a scoring opportunity

defender: a player who stops the opposing team's players from scoring, by blocking or taking possession of the ball

FIFA: acronym for the Federation Internationale de Football Association, the world governing body for association football based in Switzerland

free kick: a kick awarded to an opposition player when a player has committed a foul

friendly: a match between two teams that has no competitive value

goalkeeper: The player who is allowed to stop the ball with his hands when in the goal area

hat trick: when a player scores three goals in a single match

header: using the head to pass or control the ball

man-to-man marking: a soccer defensive system where defenders are designated one attacking player to track continuously

Glossary

midfielder: the playing position for players responsible for linking play between attackers and defenders

penalty: a kick is awarded when a foul has been committed inside the penalty area in front of the goal. A penalty is taken by one player opposed only by the goalkeeper.

penalty shootout: Method of deciding a match which has ended in a draw after full-time and extra-time. Players from each side take turns to try to score against the opposition goalkeeper.

Tiki-Taka: style of play characterised by short passing and maintaining possession. The style is primarily associated with Spanish club FC Barcelona and the Spanish National Team.

treble: when a club wins three major trophies in a single season

UEFA: acronym for the Union of European Football Associations, the governing body of football in Europe